Knights, Kings and Conquerors

20 Stories from British History

Geraldine McCaughrean was born in North London and has a degree in Education. She has been writing full time for many years and has won the Whitbread Award, the Guardian Children's Fiction Award, the Carnegie Medal and, most recently, the Blue Peter Book Award.

Knights, Kings and Conquerors is the first in a series of five books which will include all 100 stories from *Britannia: 100 Great Stories from British History*.

Knights, Kings and Conquerors

20 Stories from British History

Geraldine McCaughrean
Illustrated by Richard Brassey

TED SMART

First published in Great Britain in 2001
by Orion Children's Books
a division of the Orion Publishing Group Ltd
Orion House
5 Upper Saint Martin's Lane
London WC2H 9EA

Reprinted 2001, 2002

The stories in this volume were originally published as
part of *Britannia: 100 Great Stories from British History*,
first published by Orion Children's Books in 1999.

This edition produced for
The Book People Ltd
Hall Wood Avenue,
Haydock,
St Helens WA11 9UL

A catalogue record for this book is
available from the British Library.

Typeset at The Spartan Press Ltd,
Lymington, Hants

Printed in Great Britain
by Clays Ltd, St Ives plc

ISBN 1 85881 851 6

Contents

Since When Was History True?

You probably know all about King Arthur and his Knights of the Round Table. But how about Brutus the Trojan? Or Ludd and his bath of cold water? Or Ina the king who wouldn't retire? Once these characters, like Arthur, were household names. Their stories were handed down by word of mouth, from generation to generation. And no one stopped to ask whether or not they were true. They were just history.

Today, historians are dedicated to facts. But for most of history, history has been less about the truth than about legend, hearsay and the love of a good story.

So consume these stories with a generous pinch of salt, but remember that, to your forefathers, they were the very stuff of history.

Gogmagog and the Exiles of Troy

about 1100 BC

As the city of Troy burned, the conquering Greeks spilled Trojan blood and laid waste to the marvels of the city. But as well as looting and destroying, they took prisoners – hundreds of prisoners – and carried them back to Greece to work as slaves.

Those hundreds became, in time, thousands – generations of slaves toiling away their days in the villas and harbours and vineyards of Greek kings. Gradually, they began to forget their Trojan heritage, the glory which had once been theirs. Not Brutus. Though born a slave and the son of slaves, Brutus felt Trojan nobility boiling in his veins, and by telling the great old stories, he stirred up his fellow slaves to remember, too, and to rebel. They fought their Greek masters, broke free and ran.

That army of freed men would have followed Brutus anywhere. All their lives they had known nothing but work and whip, whip and work. Now they were drunk on liberty and looking for a homeland to call their own.

Over mountains and plains and wintry wastes of sea, Brutus led his "Trojans", until they came to the Isle of Albion, walled with white cliffs, and they set their

1

hearts on owning it. Sailing past the cliffs, and keeping offshore of the pebbly southern beaches, Brutus landed his fleet in an inviting river estuary, saying:

"Here I am and here I rest,
And this town shall be called Totnes"

(which perhaps sounded better in his native tongue).

So what if this place were peopled by giants with heads like haystacks and fists like club hammers? Nothing but slavery held any fear for Brutus's men. They were warriors, with warrior blood in their veins, whereas the giants were merely big, with fewer brains, for all the size of their heads.

By cunning and by military might, the Trojans drove back the giants, until, like bees trapped in a bottle, the last and fiercest were congregated all in one narrow isthmus of the island – in Cornwall. Largest and most ferocious of them all was Gogmagog. His temper was as hot as lava, and his belch as loud as erupting volcanoes, and he stamped so hard that the Cornish rocks under him were compressed to shiny tin.

Though they had been felling giants like so many trees, even the fearless Trojans swallowed hard at the sight of Gogmagog dancing on the Cornish hills, wielding his blunt stone hammer, singing out bloodthirsty recipes for Trojan pie.

Now in those days, battles were not a scrimmaging scrum of punches and blows and the victory going to the only men left standing. Lone champions did battle on behalf of their armies. But who could wrestle Gogmagog and live?

Only Corineus was willing to try. "I am ready!" he cried, stripping off his armour and rolling up his sleeves. "I will fight him!"

Brutus's army gave a low groan at the thought of their finest general, hero of many a battle, dying in his second-best tunic, neck broken by a grinning gargoyle of a giant. But the message went out – shouted in at every cave door and down every rabbit hole: "Corineus will fight Gogmagog, if he dares to show himself!"

As the sun rose next day, high on a headland, like a lighthouse signalling danger, a dark shape loomed up against the brightness of the sky: Gogmagog. The giant picked up a cow and ate it, throwing the bones into the wind, so that they scattered among the ranks of the Trojans. "Send out your man!" he said, "or leave this island to me and mine!" He made Corineus look like a seedling beside an oak.

But Corineus was quick and nimble. By the time Gogmagog had raised his fist to crush him, Corineus was shinning up the thongs of the giant's sandals, clambering up his tunic, swinging from his beard. And Corineus was strong, too. He could twist the hairs in a giant's ear so that tears sprang from his eyes, and when he butted his head against the bridge of the giant's nose, Gogmagog's purple eyes spun.

Corineus was light on his feet, and knew how to throw an opponent off balance or trip him from behind. Corineus swarmed over Gogmagog, wearying him with bruises, rattling him with laughter. All day they wrestled, while the bright sea winked and the seagulls screamed with excitement, and the grass wore thin on the headland. All Cornwall shook so that its smooth coastlines were made jagged by cliff-falls into the sunny sea.

But as the sun itself grew weary and dropped down the westerly sky. Gogmagog caught hold of Corineus

3

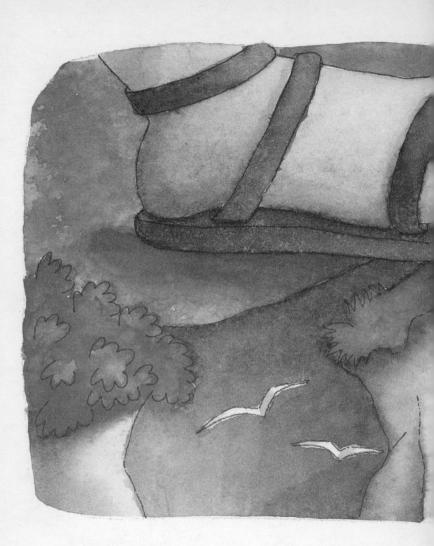

and whirled him around in the air. "Fall into the sea and be lost, you bird-dropping, you pebble, you raindrop!" he bellowed, and threw Corineus towards the sea.

Only by clinging to the grass with the tips of his fingers did Corineus save himself from plunging over the cliff-edge, and as he hung there, over the deadly drop, Gogmagog put his fists on his hips and laughed.

Pausing only to shout a string of curses at the watching Trojans, the giant lifted a foot to stamp on Corineus's fingers . . .

But at the last moment Corineus swung sideways, snatching hold of a thorn bush, and Gogmagog's foot broke off the cliff's edge, so that he pitched, bellowing and tumbling, heels over howling head, down into the sea below.

Thus Corineus won for himself the little dominion of Cornwall, and Brutus's Trojans the whole realm of Albion. The smaller, female giants, creeping out from their homes in caves and potholes and the mouldy boles of ancient trees, pleaded piteously for their lives. And the Trojans, lonely for wives, married them and bred a race of hard-working, deep-digging, tall-tale-telling sons.

Geoffrey of Monmouth, a cleric from Wales (or possibly Brittany) was a lecturer at Oxford between 1129 and 1151. In 1136 he produced *A History of the Kings of Britain*, merging folklore, legend and half-remembered facts into a sequence of events masquerading as history. Just when the country was trying to establish a sense of national identity, Geoffrey's book demonstrated that a kind of noble destiny was at work in the unfolding of history. It was accepted without quibble.

In the Middle Ages, the story of Brutus the Trojan was firmly believed to be true (possibly even by Geoffrey), but it is actually the work of some lover of the classics who wanted to make Britain as grand as Rome and Greece.

Gog and Magog are monstrous figures in the Old Testament. Every locality had its folk memories of local giants, so Geoffrey probably lent one of these a name suggestive of pagan evil and menace.

King Leir

about 800 BC

There was once a king with three daughters. Weary of responsibility, he decided to lay aside his crown and divide his kingdom between his daughters.

"Tell me," he said, calling them before him. "How much do you love me?"

"More than emeralds or pearls or rubies," said Gonerilla.

"More than any man on earth!" said Regan.

"And you, Cordeilla?" asked Leir of his third and favourite daughter. "What have you to say?"

"Nothing," said Cordeilla.

"*Nothing?*"

"I love you as much as a daughter should," said the princess, declining to flatter the old man, "and I think you will find, Father, that the world respects a king because of his title. Give that up and the world may treat you more unkindly than it does now."

Leir was cut to the quick by her coldness, but he hid his hurt behind towering rage. "I had meant to give you the best and greenest part of my kingdom. But now I shall give you nothing, you unfeeling child – no, not even so much as a dowry or a place in my home!"

So the youngest princess, for speaking the truth, was banished over the sea to Gaul, and King Leir laid aside his crown, intending to spend the rest of his life enjoying himself with his friends. (He had a great many friends – 140 knights, in fact.) "I shall come to stay with each of you in turn," he told his two dutiful daughters.

But as Leir grew older and more frail, he discovered that Gonerilla and Regan did not love him quite as much as they had vowed. They turned his friends out of doors, told him they had house-room for only twenty-five, then only ten, then just one. Their husbands seized his last remaining lands, ignoring his ranting protests.

Realizing the truth of Cordeilla's words, Leir set off, through storm and hardship, for Gaul, to ask for help. He must recover his crown and depose the villains who were devouring his country. On board the ship, dishevelled and frail, he was treated no better than a common vagrant by the crew. It was true, then, what Cordeilla had said: that it was the crown people respected and not the man wearing it. What kind of welcome would he receive from the daughter he had so wronged?

Cordeilla, however, had found real happiness. Aganippus, King of the Franks, had taken her for his wife, despite her lack of dowry, despite her banishment. He valued her for what she was, an honest, brave and virtuous woman. As Leir found, she had always loved him more than had either of the hypocrites Gonerilla or Regan. At a word, she and Aganippus mustered an army to wreak vengeance on the heartless sisters.

Gonerilla and Regan, too intent on squabbling with each other, could not hold out against the avenging wrath of the invading army, and died, along with their husbands. Leir was reinstated King of Britain, and for three happy years he reigned, a wiser and more humane king for his one disastrous mistake. When he died, Cordeilla buried him in a vault under the bed of the River Soar, and founded a city nearby – Leicester or Leir-under-the-Soar. She ruled in his place, tempered by hardship and injustice into the most tender and just of queens.

If this story reads like a fairy tale, it is no surprise. Geoffrey of Monmouth, who included it in his *History of the Kings of Britain* (about 1136) probably derived it from a folk tale – maybe not even a British one at that. His King Leir supposedly came to the throne very young, owing to the sudden death of his father Bladud in a flying accident using magical wings.

Raphael Holinshed, in his *Chronicles* of 1577, retold Geoffrey of Monmouth's story but altered minor details. Gonerilla became Goneril, Cordeilla Cordelia, Leir became Lear.

Shakespeare used the Holinshed versions for his great tragedy. But the play's comments on old age, madness and power are all Shakespeare's own. The place-name Leicester does not really have a connection with any King Leir.

The Three Plagues of Lud's Town

about 300 BC

Did you ever hear it said that troubles come in threes? They did for the people of New Troy.

Several generations after the coming of Brutus, a king was crowned whose name was Lud. His one ambition in life was to make New Troy the most beautiful city in the world. He built houses and towers, wharves and storehouses, streets and council halls, and he strengthened the walls against attack by any marauding foe. But the foes who came could not be kept out by mere stones and timber. Three plagues fell on the people of New Troy.

First came the Coranieid – out of the bottomless lakes and over the shale shores, all the way from Otherworld. They were shifting, whispering shadows, picking the mud from the walls with their long fingernails, picking the nails out of ships' hulls with their sharp little teeth. They lurked in every alleyway and hollow tree, every empty ale cask and cattle trough, armed with needle-sharp swords and butterfly nets. And no matter what plans were made to drive them out, the Coranieid always knew ahead of time, always escaped.

"If only my clever little brother Llefelys were here and not living far away," Lud said, as the Coranieid whispered like starlings in the city dusk. "He would know what to do."

The next plague was of thefts – not the odd bushel of corn gone missing, but whole warehouses of wine and grain and salted beef. Lud set guards outside every storehouse, then doubled the guard, but the thieving went on, night after night, until half their winter provisions were gone. There were no more banquets, no more fairs: only hunger and worry and aggravation at never catching the thief.

"If only Llefelys were here," Lud would say. "He would know who was doing this."

Then came the shrieks. They were terrible, chilling, ear-splitting brays which pierced the ear-drum and shivered the brain to dust. Every May Day Eve, the shrieks sounded in the sky over New Troy. Men and women fell dead, and the expressions on their faces did not bear looking at. "If only Llefelys were here," Lud said. "I must speak to him before next May Day."

The two brothers met in the middle of the sea, their ships banging rail to rail. Lud clasped his brother close. "You are good to come: I need your help."

Llefelys listened to Lud describing the three plagues. "I can tell you how to defeat the Coranieid," he said. "I have met their kind in Brittany. But we must take precautions. They sieve the words from the wind, you know, and not a whisper escapes them." He took out a long copper tube which he placed against Lud's ear. Putting his mouth to the other end, he spoke in a whisper: "Kudjj eitho wihfldnn unt er sunbumflicekr wolembluch."

Lud looked at him blankly. Llefelys took the speaking tube to the edge of the ship and poured a flagon of wine down it. With spluttered curses, out of the tube slid a sodden Coranieid. It sank out of sight in the sea. Now Lud was able to hear every word his brother said down the tube, and the fairies could not eavesdrop.

"And as for the thefts of food and drink," said Llefelys, laying aside the hearing trumpet, "that's the work of a giant. I know him well: we studied under the same apothecary. He has obviously mixed himself a potion which sends your guards to sleep, and while they sleep, he helps himself. Here's what you must do . . ."

"And as for the shriek," said Llefelys a while later, "that will cost you a pot of honey and a sail of your largest ship . . ."

Lud embraced his brother, thanked him and waved him farewell. He had the three solutions now to his three problems. "I should have liked Llefelys by my side, even so," he said to himself, and the Coranieid sieved the words out of the air and crunched them between their yellow teeth.

First Lud ordered his men to catch insects – crane-fly, mosquitoes and wasps – out of the summer air. These he crushed into a fine powder and mixed with brine. Then, when a high wind was blowing, Lud ordered the potion to be sprayed from the ramparts of New Troy, so that the air glittered with rainbow droplets. Harmless to ordinary people the infusion worked like strychnine on the Coranieid, and they could be seen shrivelling up like fallen leaves. The first plague was over.

Next Lud dismissed the guard outside the storehouses and granaries of New Troy and took their place himself. Alongside him stood a bath of cold water and his two-edged sword. At around three in the morning, a smell came to him on the breeze. At once he leapt – splash! – into the bath. The cold bit him to the bone, but it jarred him wide awake. The giant, thinking his magic perfume must have sent everyone to sleep, came whistling down the road, dragging several empty sacks. He had not even troubled to carry a weapon. At the sight of a man sitting in a bath of water, fully clothed and wide awake, the giant stopped short.

"No more of your thieving, you villainous oaf!" declared Lud, springing to his feet. The sword trembled in his chilly grasp, but the thought of his hungry people heated his temper red hot.

"All right. I shall come no more," said the giant, feeling the tip of Lud's sword against his navel, "and if you don't kill me, I'll even make good what I've taken."

"Swear it on your mother's life!" insisted Lud through chattering teeth.

"Oh, I do, I do," the giant assured him affably. "Now please let me go. It's May Day Eve tomorrow and I want to be many a mile away when that accursed shriek sounds!"

"Before you go, you can do a job of work for me," said Lud. "I want you to dig me a hole outside the city walls – a very big hole indeed."

16

So the giant dug a hole – at extraordinary speed, because he was so anxious to be gone – and Lud spread the largest sail of his largest ship over the hole to conceal it. A bowl of honey was placed on the centre of the sailcloth, and then Lud issued wax earplugs to his soldiers and plugged up his own ears.

At about midday on the May Day Eve, the shrieks sounded, far away to the north. Even so, several men and women fell dead and a water tower crashed to the ground. But instead of covering their heads with their arms, Lud and his soldiers were able, for the first time, to watch the sky. Winging towards them came two great dragons.

One was red as blood, the other white as a glacier.

And as they flew they lunged at one another, clashing wings, engulfing each other in gouts of fire and smoke. Above all they shrieked – that ear-splitting, brain-shattering shriek which had killed so many of Lud's subjects. Scales the size of shields rained down on the city. The fight was terrible to watch, and yet it was plain neither beast would win; they were doomed to fight every May Day Eve until the end of time.

At the sight of the honey, something astonishing happened. For the shrieking dragons broke off fighting, and hovered directly over the square of sailcloth. The smell seemed irresistible to them, for they circled lower and lower and came slowly in to land.

The sailcloth sank under their weight and spilled them into the pit, but the dragons barely noticed; they were too busy gorging on the honey. No sooner had they licked up the last dregs, than they fell deeply asleep, coiled round and about each other. Out from hiding raced Lud and his army of men. They folded the sailcloth over the dragons, and stitched it into a parcel. Then they carried the parcel as far as they could to the west, where they buried it in a stone-lined hole at the top of the highest mountain they could find, and filled it in with boulders and loose earth.

New Troy was restored to the peace of earlier, happier times, and such was the gratitude of the people that they renamed the town after their hero. City of Lud, they called it – Caer Luddein. And in time, blown on by wind and rain, that name was worn down into London. Lud was buried there, by Lud Gate. And if you walk to the top of Ludgate Hill, you may still see, spread before you, the city which Lud rescued from its three plagues.

The King Lud mentioned by Henry of Huntingdon in his *Historia Anglorum* (1154) had existed in many forms earlier in history. He began life as Nodens, a British god adopted by the Irish then the Welsh who told stories of Lludd-of-the-Silver-Hand. Centuries later, Lludd or Lud had become a legendary king, featuring in the great *Mabinogion* cycle of medieval Welsh stories. During the Middle Ages, a gate really did stand on Ludgate Hill, decorated with images of English kings, including Lud. Defaced, restored, improved upon, it was finally destroyed in the Great Fire. A reconstruction survived until 1760.

Though London may have derived its name from one man or a local tribe, that name was probably Londinos, or something similar. It was certainly not named after Lud.

The Tin Islands

about 100 BC

Yellow amber and purple cloth, pottery and jewellery, spices, sponges and glass: the merchants of Phoenicia had wonders to tempt the most wary. Long before the Romans came to Britain, they knew of its existence, for Phoenician merchants were bringing tin and skins and slaves from some northern island realm they referred to as "Cassiterides": the Tin Islands.

Now tin, as a constituent of bronze, was of vital importance to the Romans. They did not want to be dependent on the Phoenicians – to have to pay Phoenician prices for this valuable commodity. So they ached to find these "Cassiterides", to tap their bottomless resource of tin.

Battening on to the wake of a Phoenician trader, one Roman captain determined to follow him to his secret source. He would not let the ship out of his sight until he had found out where the Phoenician went ashore to barter for the so-called "white lead". Day and night he matched the Phoenician's speed, though the merchant was as eager to *keep* his trade secrets as the Roman was to have them. The merchant tried altering course, veering wildly about on the open ocean to give his pursuer the slip. But the Roman clung on grimly, following every tack and gybe. It terrified him, for Roman ships were coastal vessels, not built for open sea, and the Phoenician took him into grey, heaving waters very different from the sunny Mediterranean.

"So. You dog my heels, do you?" muttered the Phoenician under his breath. "Very well, I shall lead you where you have no wish to go." And he set course

for shallow water.

Perhaps he thought he knew the coastal waters well enough to pick his way through deep-water channels. Perhaps he realized that his nation's secret had to be protected at whatever cost. With a sickening, grinding judder, his vessel ran aground. Too intent on following to put about in time, the Roman vessel too lumbered

on to the hidden shoals. Within sight of one another, the two ships were quickly dismantled by pounding waves – reduced to flotsam and the cries of drowning men.

The Phoenician captain clung to a spar and kicked out for land, knees scraping on the rocks which had sunk him. The sea washed him up, limp and cold as seaweed, on a lonely beach, ship gone, cargo lost, but his life still clenched in his chattering teeth.

Months later, weary and hundreds of miles away, he found his way home. Recounting his story, he was able to report to his fellow merchants, to the governors and ministers of his home town, that the whereabouts of the Tin Islands had been kept out of Roman hands. They were not slow to show their appreciation. "You shall have the value of your cargo!" they declared. "The state awards it you for the service you have done us all!"

Inhabitants of the region now called Syria, the Phoenicians were intrepid explorers, venturing farther and farther afield in search of new markets, new commodities to sell. They were middle-men creating contact between continents and empires.

Their trading visits undoubtedly enriched the lives of the Ancient Britons. But the fact that merchants found a ready market here for luxury goods dispels the picture of Ancient Britons as primitive savages.

Phoenician trading accounts for some amazing archaeological finds within the British Isles: Roman coins predating the Roman invasion, Scandinavian amber, Egyptian glass beads . . . The above story was recorded by Phoenician chroniclers in the first century BC. It is not recorded what became of the Roman ship or its crew.

Reserves of tin are largely exhausted now, but 2,000 years ago Britain was sole supplier to a Europe clamouring for bronze tools and weaponry. It was inevitable that the Roman Empire would not rest until it had found and conquered the "Islands of Tin".

"I Came, I Saw, I Conquered"

55 BC

For a land-loving man like me from a warm, sunny city, the crossing was a nightmare. The cavalry had not even managed to set sail from Gaul because of a contrary wind. Then, just as the white cliffs of Albion came into sight, a storm blew up which split the fleet and drove half of us one way, half the other. The landing site was unsuitable, the tide was against us, and the Britons were ready and waiting for us, armed to their blue-painted nostrils.

They came screaming down the beach. The keels of our big ships were so deep that Caesar could not get in close to the shore. Do you know what a Roman soldier's armour weighs? This chain mail tabard, the bronze helmet, the leather body armour? Even in August the British sea is not clear like the Mediterranean. Looking over the side, we could not see how deep the water was or where it was safe to step. If we fell over in all that weight of armour . . .

The Britons had no such problems. Their arms and legs were bare. They waded out towards us to fight us in the surf where we were at our most helpless. They were even driving their chariots in and out of the water, raising glassy fantails of spray higher than our heads: an awesome sight.

Then the standard-bearer leapt overboard, brandishing the Eagle of the Tenth Legion. To lose that to the enemy! Unthinkable! "Leap down, soldiers!" he yelled. "Unless you want to betray the Eagle to the enemy!"

There was no more hesitating then. Men from the other ships jumped in with both feet, wallowing about like seacows, staggering towards the shore, sandals slipping on the slimy seabed.

But I was one of Caesar's reserve. He was sending us in by the boatload to wherever the line looked weakest. I and four others jumped into a little boat and rowed for an outcrop of rocks about halfway to the shore. We climbed on to it and began throwing rocks and pebbles – as good a weapon as any against half-naked men. I tell you, we pelted them like shepherd boys scaring off wolves.

Unfortunately we got isolated from the main force, and to my – er – discomfort, I realized that the tide was going out. The stretch of water separ-ating us from the beach was growing narrower and narrower; dry sand was appearing nearer and nearer to our rock. The Britons came at us with everything: rocks and chariots, spears and darts and arrows . . . The four men with me, seeing it was hopeless, jumped back into the boat and pulled away. "Come on, Scaeva!" they called. "Leave it, Scaeva!" But I had the madness of battle on me. That Eagle-bearer had inspired me, I suppose. We were within clear sight of Caesar's ship, and I did not want him to see me turn tail. So the four pushed off without me – left me standing on this pile of rocks, soaked by the waves breaking behind me, being pelted like a target at a fair. When I raised up my shield now, I could see daylight through it from the spear-holes, the axe-slashes, the tears made by their rocks and arrows.

Those chariots of theirs were terrifying: we have nothing like it. They circled me at full tilt, their wheel-hubs striking sparks from the rocks, the spray blinding me. An axe smashed my helmet, a rock hit me in the face and broke my nose: the world turned red in front of me. I used my spear first, but that was soon wrenched out of my hands. Then I used my sword. By Mars! I thought, I'll take a dozen of you down with me to the Underworld!

A sudden sharp pain in my thigh! An arrow. My sword broke like glass against a battle axe. They battered my shield out of my hand. Time to go, Scaeva, I said to myself, and I dived off the rock before the tide left me there, utterly high and dry.

Jove, that water was cold! The frigidarium at the public baths was never as cold as that sea. I could see my comrades leaning over the side of a ship, beckoning, whistling, calling my name. The sea seemed to be inside me and out, flowing through my wounds, washing the strength out of me. Arrows kept falling all round me. But at last – I hardly remember it – hands were pulling me over the rail, my blood running down into the scuppers. "My shield!" It was all I could say. "My shield!"

Once the legions were ashore, things took a different turn, of course. The men closed ranks, locked shields, formed squares, gave those barbarians a lesson in Roman warfare. Discipline.

It is discipline that makes the difference, you see: discipline and years of professional training. The enemy fled. But without cavalry, how could we give chase? Hopeless. We had just to watch them run.

"My shield!" It was all I could think of. "My shield! I lost it at the rock!" It is the ultimate disgrace for a Roman soldier (except perhaps for losing his legion's Eagle) to lose his shield. When I saw Caesar coming towards me I thought it was to reprimand me. I racked my brains for an excuse, but all words seemed to have bled away down my nose.

"What is your name?" He was speaking to me. Julius Caesar, greatest of the Romans. Better I should have drowned than come back without my shield!

"Scaeva, Caesar. Forgive me, Caesar, my shield . . ."

"Scaeva, you fought today as a Roman should. You set an example for all soldiers to follow. Such courage merits promotion, *Centurion* Scaeva."

Centurion! There is no higher honour a soldier can win than to be made a centurion for his valour. One day grandchildren, as yet unborn, will talk of it as they run their little fingers over my battered nose. My wife will write it on my memorial stone: "Scaeva: he was made centurion by Julius Caesar the day Rome conquered Albion."

But Mars deliver me from actually having to *live* in this bleak, miserable country. We are going home tomorrow, thanks be to the gods.

As conquests go, Julius Caesar's invasion on 26 August 55 BC looks remarkably like a defeat. Having captured the beach at Deal and one hill fort, exchanged hostages with the local chieftains and lost forty of his finest ships in a storm off Walmer, he packed up and sailed back to Gaul.

Back in Rome, the Senate were distinctly sceptical about what Caesar had achieved. "*Veni, vidi, vici,*" he told them. "I came, I saw, I conquered." Perhaps he should have added "*Fugi*", for good measure: "I came away at high speed."

Caesar was a great historian as well as a great commander. He kept vivid and detailed accounts of his battles, and it is he who immortalized Scaeva's heroism on the rocks.

Not for 100 years did the Romans come back to finish the job Caesar had started. Then they came with overwhelming force of arms and overran the southern coast and made sure of conquest. But still history credits Caesar with taking Britain into the Roman Empire.

The Resting Place

AD 50

There was once a hill so clad in magic that it attracted legends to it like roosting birds. The Celts called it the Island of Glass and in winter it was ringed with floodwater, so that it stood rooted in its own reflection. All around it were lesser hills, like children round their mother.

But this story begins on another hill, thousands of miles away. Joseph of Arimathea, as he stood on Golgotha Hill watching Jesus die on a wooden cross, was moved to offer his own tomb to Jesus's family so that they would have somewhere to lay His body. True, Joseph was a rich man and could afford to buy another grave, but a man does not lightly give up the resting place he has chosen for his mortal remains.

Within days, Joseph's tomb was restored to him, empty, vacated. Jesus had risen from the dead. But Joseph did not choose to reclaim his resting place. He was a disciple, now, a true believer, wandering the world, passing on to people the teachings of Jesus and the news that He had risen from the dead.

With a small band of friends, Joseph sailed for Albion. His ship navigated the Severn River, from where he travelled inland to the county called Summer Land and the cluster of hills round about the Island of Glass. The friends were all weary. Climbing a small hill

for a better view, Joseph leaned heavily on his thorn-wood staff and christened the place Weary-All Hill. From the crest, the Island of Glass was clearly visible. What a long way he had come from Golgotha to reach this green place. Joseph drove his staff into the soft, damp, autumn ground, curled up in his cloak and went to sleep.

He dreamed of wings and of light, of music and voices and ladders between the sky and the hill. "Rest *here*, Joseph," said the Angel Gabriel, hovering on kestrel wings. "Build *here*, Joseph."

On waking, Joseph told his followers, "Here is where we shall live and work."

They were not looking at him. They were staring at his staff. While they had slept, its smooth shaft had grown a dozen twiggy shoots, and small green nodules were starting to form. By Christmas it would be in blossom.

Weary-All Hill (though of God's making) actually belonged to a local nobleman. He was a busy man; he had no interest in stories of miracle-workers in far-off lands, who died and came back from the dead. Frankly, he did not believe a word of it. But the hill was too steep to farm, so he gave Joseph and his friends permission to build.

Joseph built a church out of wattle and daub – a crude, draughty place, with few comforts. But the view was second only to Paradise, and the birdsong sweeter than the singing of angels. A little religious community grew up, converts to Christianity arriving one by two by three. Joseph was content. He had found his second resting place: a good place to pass eternity. He was buried somewhere on the hill: the exact spot was soon forgotten. The wattle-and-daub church fell into ruins. But one thing lasted, as fresh and new as on the day of its coming. Each Christmas time, Joseph's thorn-wood staff would erupt into blossom – a miraculous sight. Soon people were making pilgrimage just to see the Holy Thorn. Some said it reminded them of Jesus's crown of thorns. Some said it put them in mind of life springing up new out of stark, thorny death.

Some also liked to think that Joseph had brought with him a treasure far more precious than a walking stick. It was rumoured that he had owned the room where Christ and His disciples ate their Last Supper together before the crucifixion. As the owner of the room, Joseph must, of course, have owned the crockery they used. And *that* meant he must have owned the cup from which Jesus drank, saying "Take, eat. This is my blood which is shed for you and for all Mankind."

What if Joseph had brought that cup with him to Weary-All Hill? What if he had hidden it somewhere near the wattle-and-daub church? So began the greatest treasure hunt in the history of Britain – the quest for the Holy Grail: prize beyond price, wonder beyond magic, visible only to the pure of heart.

Five centuries later, in the days of King Arthur, legend claims that the Holy Grail was found by the best of Arthur's knights.

Though Joseph of Arimathea is mentioned in the Bible, there is no solid evidence that he travelled all the way to Weary-All Hill carrying the Holy Grail. But to simple people centuries ago, such legends were accepted without question. (It was even believed that Joseph of Arimathea and Jesus had travelled to Britain in the undocumented years between the Nativity and the Christ's adult life.)

The Grail itself may have started life as a pre-Christian goal – the horn of plenty – and it certainly altered over the years thanks to inventions and mistranslations (San Grael may be a rough Latin translation of "dish" or of "holy blood".) In fact the poet T. S. Eliot said that the whole Grail tradition was a "heap of broken images" piled up over hundreds of years.

Boudicca the Firebrand

60

Her name meant "victory". Even in the good days, she looked like a firebrand, that fiery red hair tumbling down past her waist. Boudicca was married to Prasutagus, chief of the Iceni tribe on the flat lands of Norfolk. Though the Romans had conquered and colonized the entire country, they allowed many of the revered local kings to keep their thrones. So Boudicca was a queen and her three daughters were princesses. Then Prasutagus, her husband, died, and his greedy and arrogant Roman landlord decided to help himself to Prasutagus's silver plate and armoury, his chariots and cattle, his lands and power. He had Boudicca lashed to a cart and flogged till her red hair was redder still with blood. And all the while, she could hear the screams of her daughters, as laughing Roman soldiers mauled them.

What were they now? A widow and three girls, dispossessed and homeless. But Boudicca was a queen, and her daughters were princesses, and the Iceni were a warrior tribe. Boudicca spoke to her people, her voice loud and harsh.

"Do you see what meekness and tolerance bought us? Will you stand by and see your gods cast down? Your priests murdered? Your old way of life swept

away? *Your queen flogged?* Don't our holy Druids prophesy that the Romans will be swept out of this land of ours?" She lifted her face to the sky. "O Adraste, goddess of war! Tell us what you would have us do! Shall Boudicca run north and hide her children and weep? Or shall the Queen of the Iceni and her warriors march south *and take our revenge?*"

She pulled from under her cloak something large and live and struggling. The watching crowd thought at first it was a baby, but then they saw that she had hold of it by its long silken ears.

"The hare! The hare! Let the hare run!" cried the Iceni, knowing what powers of prophecy were in a running hare. Boudicca threw the animal down.

It froze, terrified, blinded by the sudden light. Then it saw a space where the crowd had parted, and bolted

for freedom. *"To the south! To the south!"* cried the
Iceni. The omen had been given. The war was under
way.

All the humiliation and resentment against their
Roman conquerors was focused on Boudicca now, and
not only the Iceni but the Trinovantes too, and all those
whipped up along the way. Rebellion kindled like a
grassfire, and a great army rallied to the chariot of
Queen Boudicca.

Sharp blades projected from both wheels of that
chariot. It cut through a rank of foot soldiers like a
scythe through ripe corn. The Romans, lulled by
peaceful years of supremacy, suddenly found their villas
in flames around them, their shops looted and
destroyed.

Colchester was razed to the ground, and the head of

Emperor Claudius' statue lopped off and thrown into the river. Hundreds died – not just Romans but anyone who had crept under their protection and begun to live in the Roman way. Murderous with hate, Boudicca was always a furlong ahead of her army, chariot blades clearing their path, her blood-curdling war cry freezing the blood.

Suetonius Paulinus, Roman governor of Britain, was far away, on the other side of the country, attempting to stamp out the subversive influence of the Druid priests. By the time news reached him of Boudicca's uprising, she had driven a wedge through the legions of Rome and rampaged south to London. He could do nothing to turn her back. The vast rambling sprawl of London could not withstand her savagery.

Over mud lanes and marble pavements Boudicca's chariot wheels rolled, and the air was so full of ash from burning buildings that her skin was spotted like a leopard's, her red hair just one more tongue of flame. Ships blazed and sank alongside the Thames wharves. And everywhere the sooty air rang with the cry:

"Boudicca! Boudicca! Victory! Victory!"

Suetonius Paulinus made his stand in the Midlands, his 10,000 men to Boudicca's 50,000. He chose a spot where three hills protected his army's back and rear flanks, and his cohorts formed squares, the sun snagging on their regimental eagles, on their standards, on their spear-points.

Such stillness they presented, in comparison with the torrent of men and women who teemed down on them. The cry of *"Boudicca!"* rang back off the faces of the hills. But the Roman cohorts were silent, except for the jingling of a horse's bridle, the beating of a single drum like a steady heartbeat.

They seemed barely human, those squares of armoured military might, every head helmeted, every face obscured. Some of the red crests of the centurions were as long as Boudicca's hair. Every long rectangular shield was locked against the shield alongside. It was like hurling water on to a box of bronze, and though Boudicca charged once, twice, a third time, she could not break those disciplined squares.

Then the cohorts began to beat on their shields with their short swords and to push forward, slicing, stabbing, routing, re-forming into squares. They came on with such ruthless certainty that the Britons turned tail and ran.

Boudicca's shrill, grating voice summoned her daughters to her chariot. She pulled them in over the tailboard. They crouched, bleeding, against her legs as she whipped up her horses to a last frenzied gallop. This time her bladed wheels cut down her own people as she fled capture.

She drove as far as the great forest of Epping – in those days a tossing, immeasurable sea of dense green trees older than either Romans or the tribes of Britain. Out of the sunlight she flashed, into its ominous shade. The Romans could not fail to follow. The trail of a battle chariot carrying four women is not hard to trace. Escape only bought Boudicca a little time: a brief respite to be alone with her daughters and to shed the bloody madness of battle.

They came to rest in a clearing where the trees stood too close and the undergrowth too dense for the chariot to pass. White and purple bell-flowers swung from twining stems among the saplings and fallen boughs.

"Remember Caractacus who fought the Romans for ten years in Wales?" said Boudicca. "First they captured his wife and children, then they took him to parade in the streets of Rome. That must never happen to us." The three girls shuddered and lowered their heads. "What do you say, children? Let's gather flowers and make a drink to refresh our flagging souls." So they picked the purple flowers and stewed them into a purple liquor. "Let us drink to Adraste, who shall give us the last victory. And as you drink, remember the prophecies of the Druids. One day these Romans will be gone, swept away and forgotten." Then she kissed her three daughters tenderly, and they all drank. Poison to make them sleep. Poison to put them beyond reach of Roman revenge.

Their bodies were never found.

Boudicca (also sometimes Boadicea) was robbed of her kingdom and humiliated at the same time as outrageous wrongs were being committed in Colchester. Veterans of the Roman army were evicting the British and forcing them to work on reconstruction of the city as well as a new temple to the dead Emperor Claudius, now declared a god. So there was plenty of support for Boudicca's rebellion.

A layer of ash has been found under present-day London which dates from her burning it down. Verulamium (St Albans) was also razed to the ground. Her body is variously reputed to lie in Hampstead, in Lincolnshire, in Epping Forest – even under Platform 10 of King's Cross Station.

Running Towards Paradise

300

His sandalled feet trod the mosaic floors depicting all the Roman immortals, but Alban's mind was filled by only one god – a god so immense and magnificent that He overflowed Alban's mind and spilled out of him in a torrent of joy. But these were times when the Roman army, in which Alban was a soldier, was still dutiful to the gods of Rome. Though Alban and his fellow legionaries were born in Britain, they occupied and policed it on behalf of Rome, and were obliged to worship Roman gods – Neptune and Jupiter, Janus and Juno and Diana. Loyal Romans purged Christians like the lice in their uniforms.

When the search party came to the house of Amphibalus, a

Christian priest fleeing persecution, they immediately arrested the man they found there. It was not until he was brought for judgement that they realized it was not Amphibalus at all, but it was a Roman in disguise. Alban of Verulamium had taken the priest's place to allow him time to escape.

The judge was incensed that Alban, who served under the Roman eagle, symbol of Jupiter, should so

deny the Roman gods. "Make sacrifice to the true gods of Rome!" he demanded, but Alban refused. "I worship only the living and true God." Neither torture nor threats could break his resolve.

"Take him out and put an end to him!" raged the judge, and Alban was led away to die. A large crowd had gathered at the place of execution, on a hilltop beyond the river. They stood speculating on what Alban had done and why. Alban was so eager to keep his appointment with immortality that, instead of walking to the bridge, he hurried straight down to the riverbank. The tumbling water slid to a halt, evaporated, and was gone, leaving him a dry path to cross over. Minutes later he crested the hill and crossed as easily from life to death, his head slashed from his shoulders by a Roman sword.

"Let that set an example to any other Roman who thinks to abandon the gods of Olympus!" said the judge, watching from his window.

It did set one, too. For Alban was happy to die. Roman soldiers had always been ready to die for the Roman eagle, for Caesar, for their honour, but they had never loved their gods enough to die like that: fearless, happy, eager to set out on the road to paradise. Alban was Roman Britain's first martyr. And martyrs make for converts.

During the fourth century, Christianity swept Roman Britain, until it was the predominant religion. When the Roman Empire crumbled and the Roman armies withdrew from Britain, they left behind them a Christian country.

Then the Danes came, under their raven-banner. The Vikings and the Danes arrived in longships, burned down the monasteries, slaughtered the monks, stole the crucifixes and tore up the Gospels. They brought with them their own gods: Thor and Odin, Wotan and Freya – gods who admired bloodshed and awarded paradise only to warriors. The few Christians who survived the rout fled west into Wales and Ireland, leaving the stones of their churches to be re-used for pagan temples or swallowed up once more by primeval forest. Their villages were lived in now by the pagan, blond-haired, blue-eyed Angles.

ALBAN

According to the Venerable Bede, Christianity
had already made inroads in Britain when
Emperor Diocletian came to power in Rome
and launched a massive persecution.

Alban may not have been a soldier, after all,
but more of a civil servant in the walled city of
Verulamium, but he did exist. He was
beheaded in about the year 300, on the hilltop
where St Alban's Abbey now stands. (Five
centuries later, King Alfred renamed
Verulamium "St Albans".)

In 313, when Emperor Constantine turned
Christian, the persecution stopped.

The Hallelujah Victory

429

"Help us! help us!" they begged. "save us! You know the mind of God, Father! When will He help us?"

Bishop Germanus thought they were talking about their immortal souls, but they were not at all. The Britons he had come to visit were talking of their homes, their wives, their children. "We write to Rome, but they send no troops to help us, and we – God forgive us – we have forgotten all the arts of war we ever knew!"

The Roman legions had been withdrawn from England, as the Roman Empire shrank and disintegrated. For centuries the occupying forces had defended the land, fortified its borders, kept at bay all interlopers and barbarians. But now the Romans were gone, leaving the door to Britain banging open in the wind.

Scenting rich pickings, the Picts and Scots seized their chance – hardy, unconquered people who could fight with all the skill which the southern Britons had forgotten. They launched more and more audacious raids, burned villages, took cattle, killed anyone who stood in their path. "Now they are coming in hundreds – and with Saxons among them – and how shall we stand against them?" they begged the visiting bishop.

"Do as I say, and all may be well," Germanus told

the Britons, though secretly his heart quailed when he thought what the future might bring the people of the southern kingdoms.

The people did as Germanus instructed. They took their stand on high ground, on three sides of a valley – well strung out – a laughably small number in the face of the advancing army of Picts and Scots and Saxons.

On came the raiders, shaggy as beasts, silvered over with the glint of axeheads, spearheads, arrowheads, swords. They filled up the valley like a summer brook swelling into a winter river. The noise of their feet, their baggage, their ugly nasal languages rose up unmuffled by distance. Then, at a signal – the slow silent arc of a single arrow – the Britons did as they had been told to do. They opened their mouths and shouted:

"Hallelujah!"

An avalanche of sound tumbled into the hollow, bounded and resounded around, redoubled by the kettle-hollow basin of the place, echoing, re-echoing, as if the Day of Reckoning had come and a million angels were all shouting:

"Hallelujah!"

The second cry met with the first and swelled it, ricocheted around the reverberating rocks till there was more sound in the valley than air, and all of it the one word:

"Hallelujah!"

The men below turned and fled. They thought that all their enemies must have united as never before, congregated around this one valley to ambush and destroy them. And they fled. Not a stroke was struck, never an axe fell, but the Scots and Picts were routed as totally as if God had taken up arms against them.

St Germanus was the Bishop of Auxerre in France. He visited Britain in 429 to argue against a heretical Christian schism, but is better remembered for helping win the bloodless "Hallelujah Victory".

The site of the battle, Maes Garmon in Flintshire, North Wales, means "the field of Germanus".

Hengist, Horsa and the Lovely Rowena

449

After the Scots and the Picts came the Jutes,
sweeping in like the sea. There was no
stopping the relentless push westwards of
these Germanic hordes urgent for land,
greedy for the rich orchards and fields
and vineyards of Kent.

King Vortigern, already plagued
by attacks from northerners, saw the
forces of Hengist and Horsa closing
on his coastline and knew that the
Jutes were too strong for him. He did
not fall on his knees and pray. He did
not reach for his sword either. He
saw another way of surviving. Why
should he not *ally their power* to his?

Perhaps it was cowardice, perhaps
it was cunning, but Vortigern went
down to the shore and greeted the
brothers, chieftains of the Jutes: "Ah!
Just the men I need!"

He pitted Hengist and Horsa against
the Picts and Scots, saying he would pay
them if they were victorious. (He was

secretly hoping they would kill each other and leave Kent in peace.) But the Jutes easily defeated the northerners. And as soon as they had, they returned, palms outstretched for their pay. And on top of money they wanted land. What they could not get by threats, they took by force, and far from sailing away over the horizon, more of their kith and kin began to arrive.

On board one Jute ship was Hengist's daughter, Rowena. One sight of her, and Vortigern's soul was in thrall. For those blue eyes, for that yellow hair, for that

tall, willowy form, he would have sold the sun out of the sky, the salt out of the sea, anything that was his or not his to give. In exchange for Rowena's hand in marriage, he gave Hengist the throne of Kent.

Perhaps he knew it was lost already, that it was Hengist's for the taking. But there were those who thought him a traitor. Not least his sons.

Dispossessed of their inheritance, shamed by their father's marriage, Vortimer and his half-brother took up the fight which Vortigern had let fall. They rallied the men of Kent fleeced and scattered by the Jutes, and at the Ford of the Eagles clashed with such a clamour that the river water shivered like broken glass.

Horsa, the brother of Hengist, fell at the hands of Vortimer, and Vortimer's brother fell at the hands of Hengist.

Rowena's blue eyes swam with tears when the news came from Aylesford. "I weep that your dear son is dead," she told her British husband. But in truth, her Jute heart howled for vengeance at the death of her uncle, Horsa, and with misery that the Jutish fleet was even now sailing away in defeat.

Biting her tongue, Rowena awaited her chance. She paid a servant to poison young Vortimer's food and, when he died, wept crocodile tears over his grave.

"Invite my father to come back," she crooned as she consoled her grieving husband. "The time is past for wars. The land has drunk blood enough. Let us make peace, the men of Kent and the men of Jute. Do, I beg you."

So a great feast was arranged between the chieftains of Britain and Hengist's warriors.

"Let there be no weapons brought," said Hengist,

"for we shall sit down as friends and hospitality forbids that those who eat together should bear arms."

"Naturally," said Vortigern. "The laws of hospitality are the same the world over."

It was a feast to stretch the powers of the chroniclers who wrote of it. The fire spits bent under the weight of roasting meat. After such a meal, there were many oaths sworn of undying friendship and never-ending peace. "Is not Britain large enough for all of us?" cried Vortigern, face flushed, unsteady on his feet, fingers clumsy in his wife's yellow hair. "Shall we not put the killing behind us?"

Hengist too pulled himself to his feet. He did not seem to have drunk so deep. "Now, men," he said, without raising his voice. And from under their cloaks, from out of their boots, from hidden sheaths and false pockets, the Jutes drew their daggers.

Rowena looked on, unmoved, unafraid. She stretched wide her sea-blue eyes, so as not to miss a single death. No tears fell from her blue eyes.

No dagger was turned on Vortigern, for he was beneath contempt, already shackled to his enemies by love of a woman. Overturning his chair, clutching his misery to him in trembling hands, he fled, calling to Rowena to follow. But she did not. When 300 Britons lay dead on the floor, Rowena raised her glass to the ghost of Horsa and wished him peace in his warrior heaven.

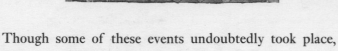

Though some of these events undoubtedly took place, they are told in such a storybook way that legend has clearly taken over from fact. Vortigern simply means "over-chief", and it is possible that there was not one, but many vortigerns who opted to collaborate with the Saxons in the hope of retaining some power in their own country. Just as appeasement did not work for Vortigern, it did not work on a grand scale either.

The Britons were driven west into Wales, Cornwall and Brittany: similarities still exist between the three languages/dialects.

One of the most bizarre claims of this legend is that the 300 murdered Britons were buried on Salisbury Plain in a mass grave over which Stonehenge was raised as a memorial. Sadly for legend, Stonehenge had been there a good 2,000 years beforehand.

The Castle Which Could Not Stand

about 450

Vortigern was desperate, hunted like a fox across the length and breadth of his own kingdom by the enemy he had thought to befriend. Holding his life in his teeth, holding his power in sweating hands, he finally found himself with his back to the Welsh mountains. There he made his stand. Planting his foot on the crest of Dinas Emrys, he commanded, "Build me a castle! You men, quarry. You men, heave. Build me a fortress!" He thought that if he built the walls high enough, both his crown and his life would be safe inside.

But though every day Vortigern's castle grew, by night it crumbled into a pile of rubble. The wind blew dusty mortar into Vortigern's open mouth. "Find me a prophet! Find me out what evil magic is eating away at my castle!" he demanded.

Superstitious advice poured from his wise men. "Your castle will not stand, my lord, until the noble blood of a fatherless boy is spilled on the foundations."

"Find one, then, and split him!"

The countryside was scoured, but though there were many children whose fathers had died, or gone away to war, there was not one who had *never had a father*.

"Who's this?" sneered Vortigern when a brown-eyed

boy was at last brought before him.

"His mother entered a nunnery the day her child was born," his advisors told him. "The child was brought up by his grandfather – a magician."

"But who was his *father*?" Vortigern wanted to know.

The child did not answer, but his mother did. "Something between a dream and a nightmare," she said, unashamed. "One night I dreamt of a man wearing a golden crown. He fathered my child, then melted away with the daylight."

The little boy stared at the woman wearing the nun's habit. This was the first time he had seen his mother, and the first he had heard tell of his dream-father. Now,

in this moment of discovery, he was to die.

"Bind him and slit him and let his blood flow!" cried Vortigern. "Tonight my castle will not fall down!"

"It will and it shall, while you build it there!" The boy's voice was high, but clear and loud. It captured every ear. "Don't you know what lies beneath this ground?"

The King snorted. "Nothing. Who knows? The ruin of something Roman." (Indeed, there were signs of ancient building, mossy with mould.) The wise men were asked, but the wise men did not know.

"Then I shall tell you," said the boy. "I have dreamed this place, and the future will come of it. Below here lies a pool of water, and at the bottom of the pool, two stone tanks. Unless you drain the pool, you may as well build on quicksand."

A muscle in Vortigern's cheek twitched. Silence hung over his army of builders until at last he spoke: "Look and see. We can kill him after."

They broke up the ground with picks. It fell away into a hollow place beneath, splashing into water. They laid bare a vast man-made basin, a sink of black water, and pumped it out down the mountainside. As the water drained away, two stone vaults the shape of coffins were uncovered.

"Inside each is a dragon," said the boy. "I have dreamed them, and the future will come of it. Wake the dragons if you dare, King Vortigern; they will tell you your fate."

"If anything were ever living in there, it is certainly dead by now," sneered Vortigern, and had his men set to with cold hammers.

The coffins broke like eggs hatching. Out of the first

came a red dragon, writhing, the colour of blood. Out of the second came a white dragon, the colour of frost. Their tails intertwined, then they turned on each other and fought. The white dragon was low and slinking: it overturned the red and scuttled for its throat. But the red dragon was leaping lively. It threw off the white one, blinding it with scarves of scarlet smoke. Then, with a lunge, the red jaws fastened on the white throat till its fire was out.

As the vanquished dragon dragged itself back into the crater to die, the red victor leapt skywards. It passed so close to Vortigern that its claws tore his cloak and its hot breath singed his beard. The horror of it rooted him to the spot.

"I have dreamed this fight, and the future will come of it," said the fatherless boy. "The red dragon represents the Britons, Vortigern: the men you betrayed to Hengist and Horsa. The white dragon is the invading horde you have brought down on us. For a time they will triumph over us, but the Britons will drive them out, as you yourself have been driven out. Uther Pendragon will rule after you are dead. The Jutes and Saxons are coming after you, Vortigern, but beyond them, behind them comes an Age of Gold!"

Vortigern's whole army turned and looked across the plain. The sun flashed off some distant metal – a spearhead? a helmet? an army?

"The pit is drained. The dragons are gone. Fill in the hole and start building, you idle dogs!" The King would have liked to cut the boy's throat and silence his prophesying. But there was not a man there who would have been ready to do it. There was magic in the lines of his small hands and in every word he spoke. "What is your name, you with the Devil for a father?"

But this time the boy's mother spoke for him. "My son's name is Merlin."

Vortigern's castle was never finished. Though its foundations were sure, so too was the future. The Jutes killed him, and buried him in a pit. And the Britons rallied under Uther Pendragon. Dragon-headed Uther, they called him, because there was fire in his blood and magic in his eyes. His best friend was Merlin the Druid, Merlin the Magician, and it was to him that Uther entrusted the safety and education of his son: the Once-and-Future-King, Arthur.

A blood sacrifice, such as the "wise men" recommended, was common practice when building in pre-Christian times and in the early centuries AD. The remains of human sacrifices have been found among the foundations of Cadbury Castle in Somerset. In some versions of this legend, the boy is not Merlin but Ambrosius or Emrys Gwledig, and Vortigern, shaken by the affair of the dragons, makes Emrys king of western Britain. Emrys later executes Vortigern for his unpatriotic deeds.

Fragments of all kinds of earlier folklore are in evidence here. The dragons are, of course, the dragons buried by Lud (see page 20). Merlin is a Celtic bard or Druid – a prophet figure who was only incorporated into the Arthurian legends later.

In truth, the Britons were ultimately driven west off their lands, dispossessed utterly by Jute and Saxon invaders.

St David and the
Naked Ladies
519-589

Arriving in the Vale of Roses in the west of Wales, St Patrick looked round him and thought, "I shall settle here." But an angel, stooping hawk-like out of a cloudless sky, urged him on his way. "This place is meant for David," said the angel, "and David is not yet born!" So St Patrick pressed on to Ireland and won it for Christ. For fifty years the Vale of Roses stood waiting.

By the time David arrived there, though, to found a monastery, the area lay at the mercy of a brutish man called Boia and his equally brutish wife. David and his monks wanted only to farm the land and to pray, but Boia wanted them gone. He set out from home, blustering and boorish, telling his wife he meant to run them off his land.

When he came back, he was meek and mild, speaking of 'joy', saying he was sorry for his sinful life. He had met David, and he was a changed man.

"Get you up there and tell that blanket-tossed son of a mangy dog to shift his bag of bones off our grazing!" squawked his wife, but Boia only looked at her with faraway eyes and a wistful smile. "They are my brothers-in-Christ, wife," he said.

So she boxed his ears and took matters into her own hands. Summoning her serving maids she told them, "Over there yonder stands a barn of a place full of lonely men, all priding themselves that they can live without wives and sweethearts, all sworn to shun women till their dying day. Get up there in your nothing-at-alls. When those monks see what they are missing, they will break their vows, and give up religion!"

The maids went – big buxom girls, with blushing cheeks and curvy bodies which they flaunted outside David's window. "Come out, saintly David, and see what you be missing by living the single life! There's kisses a-plenty out here!" They perched themselves on gates. They lounged against door posts. They rang the monastery bell and peeped in at the alms window. "Oh, *do* come out and look us over, boys! There are arms out here just waiting to hold you close!"

David saw them, and his mouth set in a hard, straight line. He kept on at his work. He behaved as if the naked ladies were no more of a nuisance than the sheep which roamed about the monastery buildings pushing their noses in at the doors. He outstared their brazen winks. He resisted their beckoning fingers. "The joys of this world, brothers, are no match for the joys of heaven," he told his monks.

And because he resisted the ladies, the other monks were able to do the same. For all the hardship of their solitary life, they loved God and their abbot enough to shun the pink maid-servants of Boia. Why, they had seen sights far more wonderful! They had seen flat ground heave itself upwards into a hill when David spoke, so that the crowds might hear him better. They

had seen springs burst out of the ground at his command. They had seen the waters at Bath bubble hot with healing grace after David's blessing. They had seen the sick healed, and barbarians like Boia transformed into gentle lambs. His maid-servants could offer them nothing so miraculous. The girls shivered in the cold, put on their clothes and went home.

In time, Boia and his neighbours had cause to be glad they had not driven David out of the Vale of Roses. Famous for his wisdom and goodness, David made his little, sleepy corner of the world famous. He made it wise with his saintly wisdom, and peaceful by his saintly example. But not till after his death did David do them the greatest favour of all. Even from beyond the grave, he brought them victory over the Saxons.

In huge marauding hordes the Saxons came, and in

skirmish after fray they fought the Britons. Though David was a man of peace, and would never have raised up a sword in anger, he gave his neighbours the best advice. "Wear a leek in your caps," he said.

"A leek?"

"A leek. There is nothing so Welsh as a leek, and the Saxons have no understanding of the magnificent nature of a leek."

It would be a badge – a mark by which a Briton, in the whirling madness of battle, could instantly recognize a fellow Briton. A man half-crazed with battle fever, half expecting at every second the slash of a blade to catch him unaware, lashes out at everyone who comes near. But in the great battle of 640, the Britons stuffed leeks in their caps, just as St David had taught them to do, and knew each other instantly on the battlefield. The Saxons (perhaps because they wore no distinguishing badge, perhaps because the prayers of St David confounded them) inflicted terrible wounds on each other and were defeated.

After the battle, the Welsh offered up thanks to St David (though he had been sleeping peacefully in his grave in the Vale of Roses for fifty years), named the day for him and declared David the patron saint of Wales.

According to legend, David was the son of a Welsh prince, Sant, born in Dyfed and educated for the priesthood in Caerleon. But David began his spiritual career in earnest on the Isle of Wight, preaching and disputing. He led a life of self-denial, and travelled to such holy sites as Jerusalem and Glastonbury. Returning to Caerleon, he eventually became archbishop of the community, moving it to the site now called St David's. St David's Day, 1 March, is commemorated by the wearing of daffodils (and leeks).

"Not Angles but Angels"
597

Within the market place in Rome, slaves were just another commodity. Listless and afraid, chained and herded, they were on a par with the penned pigs or the chickens hung up by their feet. They were on sale. They were thirsty, too, under the hot Italian sun, and the flies pestered them. Among them today were foreign slaves whose blond hair glistened and glinted in the strong sunlight – an unusual sight among the swarthy, brown- and red-haired Romans.

Brother Gregory, walking through the market, commented to his companion on the beauty of the blond-haired slave children. "What is their nation?" he asked.

"They are Angles, Brother, from Britain."

"Not Angles but angels," joked Gregory. "They have angelic faces. Are they Christians?"

"No, Brother."

"What is the name of their king?"

"King Ella," came the reply.

"Then Ella-lujah shall be sung in their land!" quipped Gregory and his companion laughed indulgently. Gregory liked to pun. Fortunately, his sense of humour was not the best thing about him.

Gregory was renowned throughout Rome, not for his jokes but for his goodness and charity; he had the ear of the Pope himself. So taken was he with the angelic appearance of those Angle slaves that he went to the Pope now and asked to be sent as a missionary to convert their pagan island to Christianity. The Pope could not spare him – he knew that Gregory was loved too much within the city for him to risk martyrdom in God-forsaken Angle-Land. His request was refused.

But Gregory remembered those blond-haired, blue-eyed children – nursed the memory even after the Pope was dead, even after Rome had elected *him* to the highest office in the world. Pope Gregory the Great

summoned a Benedictine monk called Augustine and told him, "Take forty monks and travel to England with the good news of Christ!"

Halfway there, the forty lost their nerve. They wrote asking to come home, but Gregory answered them with a letter of such eloquence and fiery inspiration that they forged onward. Armed with a silver cross and a picture of Christ crucified, Augustine landed near Ramsgate, and invited King Ethelbert of Kent to hear him preach.

The King agreed to meet them, but only in the open air, wary of the evil magic that might be practised on him indoors.

Augustine used no evil magic. Even so, within months Kentishmen and women were flocking to hear the Benedictines preach and to be baptized. Soon after Ethelbert himself knelt at Augustine's feet for baptism, one thousand of his subjects were baptized in a single day. In pairs they waded out into the River Swale, one sinking the other beneath the water as Augustine bellowed his blessing from the bank. Whole families walked into the Swale that day and waded out again Christians.

Saint Augustine's task of conversion was made considerably easier by the fact that Ethelbert's French queen, Bertha, was a Christian before he arrived. That was why he chose to land in Kent.

Ethelbert showed extraordinary tolerance in letting Augustine preach a rival religion. He was slow to be convinced himself, but allowed the Benedictines to found a monastery near Canterbury, and let his wife worship there. Once converted, he made an energetic Christian, founding St Paul's Cathedral in London in 604. After his death, however, his successor rejected Christianity, as did neighbouring kingdoms.

King Arthur and his Questing Knights

6th century

King Arthur's fabled court at Camelot stood on the fringes of the Summer Land, not far from the Island of Glass. Raised and educated by the prophet-magician Merlin, and armed with a magical sword Excalibur, Arthur set about freeing his kingdom from evil and the forces of darkness. To that end, he assembled the finest knights in the land. So that they would not quarrel

about which of them was the grandest or highest ranking, he seated them at a great round table.

Giants and dragons were slaughtered, maidens were rescued and quests were mounted. But the greatest quest of all was to find the Holy Grail.

An image of that cup, which Christ had used at the Last Supper, which Joseph of Arimathea had brought to the Summer Land and hidden in a secret place, which none but the pure of heart would be allowed to find – showed itself one feast-day to the knights of the Round Table. Immediately the knights took it for a sign that they should go questing in search of the real thing.

Sir Gawain searched, but gave up. Sir Lancelot searched, but could not find it because his heart was not pure enough. But Galahad his son, along with Sir Bors and Sir Perceval, came at last to the mysterious

castle of Corbenic, where, in a radiance of light, Jesus Christ Himself appeared to them. Amid the sound of English birdsong, Christ gave them bread and wine, then entrusted them with the very cup from which they had just drunk: the Holy Grail.

The happiness of that moment broke Galahad's heart like a loaf of bread; Perceval devoted himself to a life of prayer, and Bors returned to recount the story to his fellow knights.

But the Golden Age of King Arthur was over within a few short years. In gathering together all the good knights, Arthur had driven the forces of evil to unite in a single, menacing army. The fate of Albion had to be settled by one last battle.

In the water-threaded Summer Lands, man by man, the knights of the Round Table fought and died. The black-armoured knights of treachery and sin and greed were all killed, but at terrible cost. Only the good Sir Bedivere was left standing and, lying wounded at his feet, Arthur, clenching the last minutes of his life like sand in his fist.

"Carry me to those woods," he told Bedivere. "There is something I must do before I die." A stretch of water glinted through the trees. Arthur was desperate to reach it, but his wounds were too deep. "Take my sword," he told Bedivere. "Take Excalibur, and throw it into the water."

"*Excalibur?*" Bedivere was appalled.

He stood by the waterside, his feet in the soft, oozing black mud, and the sword in his hands. But the sheer beauty of that shining blade, that elaborate jewelled hilt, seemed far too marvellous to sink in fathomless muddy water.

He hid the sword and went back.

"What did you see when you threw it?" asked Arthur.

"I saw the moorhens run and the ripples spread," said Bedivere with a shrug.

"Then go back and take the sword from where you hid it and *do as I commanded you!*" raged the King, his eyes bloodshot with fury.

Bedivere meant to do it, he really did. He ran to the reeds and pulled out Excalibur. But the sword had such memories for him – such happy memories! Soon Arthur would be dead. Was there to be nothing left to show for the court of Camelot, the Golden Age? Again he hid the sword, and hurried back, fearful the King would die alone.

"What did you see?" whispered Arthur.

"I saw the fish scatter and the reeds shake."

"*Villain! Traitor! Liar! Must I do the job myself?*" Arthur tried to get up, but fell back in agony. Bedivere took to his heels and ran – back to the waterside, scrabbling in among the reeds. Swinging the sword round his head, he flung it, letting fall a sob of effort and misery.

But just before the expected splash, a woman's hand rose from the heart of the lake and caught Excalibur by the hilt. Three times it brandished the blade, slicing the moonbeams. Then Arthur's sword sank, drawn down out of sight.

Arthur saw from Bedivere's face that his order had been carried out, his loan repaid to the Lady of the Lake. He sank into semi-consciousness, and Bedivere knelt over him, listening for the King's last breath.

Then the sound of oars behind him made him start

to his feet. Through the trees came three women, veiled and with their hands drawn up inside their broad sleeves.

"So. It is time," they said to Bedivere. "He has earned his rest." They carried the King, with the greatest ease, aboard a low black craft moored among the reeds.

"Where are you taking him?" cried Bedivere distractedly. "Have some pity, won't you? Let him die in peace!"

"Die?" said the women. "He is sleeping. After such a life, is he not entitled to sleep? When Albion needs him, he will come back, never fear." Then each woman took hold of an oar and they rowed away, into the veiling vapours which evening had drawn up from the sodden landscape.

And where did they take him? To Avalon. A land of magic.

But where is Avalon? Why, it is the Island of Glass, of course. Or if not that island, some place very like it.

When Bedivere retraced his steps, the battlefield still lay strewn with dead. But the Knights of Arthur were all gone – all gone to Avalon to sleep alongside their king, heads pillowed on blossom petals from the Holy Thorn, sipping, in their dreams, from the Holy Grail, until their next summons to arms.

These days, the waters have drained away from the Island of Glass. But the hill is the same hill, the earth of the hill the same earth, the secrets of the hill the same well-kept secrets. Kestrels still hover, and the magic still clings.

A Romano–British war-lord named Arturus, living in the west of England, is mentioned in Welsh chronicles, a fighter of notable courage against invading Saxons.

Most Arthurian legends originate, however, from the Age of Chivalry in the eleventh and twelfth centuries, when various "literary" writers recreated him in a complex cycle of stories, none of which is likely to be true. They required a Christian figure of courtly character, pitting himself against evil. There had to be a romantic element – romantic love was just being invented – and a code of knighthood (which did not even exist in the era when Arthur supposedly lived). A body of ancient Celtic myths has become interwoven with the Arthurian legend. In it Merlin is an important figure.

Extensive efforts have been made to site Camelot, but these are driven more by romantic wishful thinking than archaeological probability.

Fleeting Glory
726

"A ship! A ship has struck the rocks, Father!" cried the fisherman's daughter above the howling wind. Dafyd leapt up and ran outdoors. The wind which met him was full of sea spray and cries, and fragments of rigging like twigs blown off a tree.

The ship in the bay lay on its side, surf crashing down on it like fists. "Help me, with the rowing boat!" Dafyd told his daughter, "or many a good man will drown tonight!"

Twenty men they dragged from the water by the scruff of the neck. Each frozen face spluttered thanks in some strange, un-Welsh tongue. At last the hulk settled and disintegrated under the strengthening daylight. Dafyd sent his daughter over the hill to fetch a monk to speak words over the dead.

Back at the hut, huddled by the fire, one of the survivors in particular seemed to command the respect of the others. All eyes were on him when he spoke.

"Reckon he's the captain," said Dafyd to his wife, "for all he doesn't look much."

The monk laughed at the simplicity of the fisherman. "O ignorant man! Do you not know English when you hear it spoken?" he said, and went to ask this "captain" who he was. A moment later he came reeling back and sat down on a crab pot. "By the saints!" he

gasped (in Welsh). "D'you know what you've done, Dafyd? You've only saved the King of Wessex, that's all! You've only rescued King Ine of Wessex!"

"Oh yes?" responded the fisherman dubiously. "And where's Wessex, then?"

King Ine, spared from an early death, spent a great deal of time at his prayers after that. He founded a church on that bleak Cardiganshire coast, in thanksgiving, and he was an altogether devout and Christian king. His queen was equally saintly, and looked forward to the time when (as was the practice in those days) King Ine would resign his crown to a younger man and live out his life in prayer and contemplation.

She was to be disappointed. Ine might be a good king, but he was also a persistent one. Having grown used to power, he did not welcome the idea of giving it up. "Another month or two," he told his wife. "Just until I am content they can manage without me." But the months passed and still Ine held the reins of power, forever travelling from castle to castle, forever checking that his orders were being carried out.

After one particularly lavish night of feasting, he once again set out for yet another corner of the kingdom. He grumbled when the Queen asked them all to turn back. "There is something I forgot," she said.

"I have things to do. Affairs of state! You really must not delay like this, wife," Ine complained, but the Queen insisted. They retraced their steps to the castle.

The banners and pennants had gone from the walls. The minstrels had been paid off and gone. Litter from the feast lay strewn around the yard and the great hall, and dogs were chewing on bones amid the dirty strewings. Chickens pecked up and down the long table where, the night before, roast swans had stood amid custards and sweetmeats. Worst of all, on the couch where King Ine and his Queen had reclined to eat, a gigantic sow was lying on her side with a dozen piglets suckling.

"Someone will pay for this!" raged Ine. "Is this the esteem I am held in? Who is responsible for this disgrace?" He glanced around him at the carls and serfs, but they only looked at the Queen.

"What's the matter, my lord?" she asked innocently. "Did you expect to leave a trail of lasting glamour behind you, after you were gone? Did you think one night's pomp and splendour would fend off dirt and decay for ever? Our feast last night was like the rule of a good king – one brief span of glory. But everything passes. Everything decays. Every king will one day be reduced to a pile of forgotten bones. Life is so fleeting."

Many men, when lectured by their wives like this, would have called it nagging. But standing there in that squalid hall, Ine suddenly glimpsed the scale of eternity, and the absurdity of kingly pomp. His lifetime was nothing but one grain of sand in a sand dune of lives, and he had already wasted too much of it fretting about detail.

So although Ine realized that his queen had deliberately staged the pigs, the dogs, the litter, he took her lesson to heart. Soon afterwards, he resigned his crown to a younger man. He made a pilgrimage to Rome, then cut off his hair, and lived like a poor peasant for the rest of his life, working with his hands, thinking, praying and, of course, talking to his wife about the things which really matter.

Ine's life and forty-year reign is recounted by the
Venerable Bede in his *Ecclesiastical History of the
English People*.

Apparently the King did much to organize the
structure and practices of the Church, and
established a code of law. During Ine's pilgrimage to
Rome, he founded a church there, as well as a school
for the education of English boys. The money was
raised by levying a tax of one penny on each
household in Wessex. The people grumbled
considerably. Ine's abdication threw England into
years of bloody war.

Offa's Shame
794

It is only natural that a bridegroom should be nervous. But as King Ethelbert stepped out-of-doors and walked towards his horse, his legs shook, he staggered and almost fell. The waiting horses bolted, sending wedding gifts and bundles of clothing tumbling to the ground. Thatching slumped from the roofs. It was not Ethelbert who was trembling, but the earth itself. Dust rose so thickly that, for an hour, night returned.

"It is a bad omen, son," said his mother. "Do not go to Mercia!"

The King of East Anglia laughed. "It would be bad luck indeed not to marry the fairest maid in Christendom! When I take the Princess Alfleda for a wife, Anglia shall be united with Mercia and I shall be the happiest of men. If this is an omen, Mother, it is sent to some greater man than me."

Meanwhile, in the next-door kingdom, another woman wept and turned her face to the wall. "I tell you my poor heart will break! I shall never know another moment's happiness if this wedding takes place!"

King Offa slapped his forehead. "But what would you have me do, lady? My word is given! The betrothal is made. My daughter Alfleda is promised to Ethelbert. He is on his way here to marry her, even now! Why should they not wed?"

Pale and anguished, Queen Drida dabbed away tears. "It should be enough that I ask it," she said, and bit her beautiful blood-red lip.

A hundred miles away, sleeping on the cold ground under a snow shower of stars, King Ethelbert screamed in his sleep. He dreamed that his mother stood at the foot of a big double bed, weeping tears of blood. The tears splashed on to the sheets of the bed, while an armed man swung an axe over and over again, splintering the canopy, the legs, the footboard, splitting the mattress till the air was snowy with feathers. He knew it was his bed, too: his bridal bed.

Never before had the spoiled Queen Drida striven so hard to get her way. It made her sulky that Offa begrudged her what she asked. "Alfleda is too good for this yokel king!" said Drida. "There are far greater men over the ocean for her to marry. I will not have her wasted on a fenland peasant!"

"Silence, Drida," said Offa. "I have accepted the man's gifts and promised him my daughter's hand. Say no more about it. My mind is made up."

Queen Drida did hold her tongue – bit into it with sharp little teeth and kept silent. But the ambition did not die within her, nor her determination to stop the marriage.

White-faced for want of sleep, grimy and dishevelled from his journey, King Ethelbert of Anglia smiled broadly at the sight of Offa's castle. Here was the home of his beautiful bride. Tomorrow he would marry Alfleda. He was a truly lucky man.

As he stepped in at the door of Offa's throne room, he hesitated. There was an uneasy atmosphere. The Queen was looking steadfastly at the floor. But Offa opened his arms in welcome, beaming with delight:

"Come in, son-in-law! Come in and welcome!" Two long tables groaned under joints of meat, custards, sweetmeats and cakes. Ethelbert took his place at the feast, and Alfleda sat down beside him, birdlike and delicate. The double doors closed against the weather, and a bolt shot home.

Hours later, flushed with wine and laughing with joy, Ethelbert was shown to his room by the Queen. It was luxurious, with a curtained bed, tapestries on the wall and, at the centre of the room, a vast chair piled with down-filled cushions. Ethelbert thanked the Queen over and over again: "Such a welcome . . . such a feast . . . such a fine, comfortable room." This was the last night he would retire to bed alone: tomorrow he would be sharing his dreams with the lovely Alfleda. Weary and overfed, he flung himself down in the great chair.

Lurching backwards and sideways, the chair twisted and buckled. Then it plunged through a jagged hole in the thin planks which had been supporting it. Down it fell into darkness, into the musty, hollow darkness of a hidden well. Ethelbert saw the room's light recede to a smaller and smaller circle, then the chair struck the bottom of the well and splintered under him. The fall broke his bones, knocked all the wind out of him. But finding himself alive, Ethelbert began to yell for help.

He was heard, too. Queen Drida's hired men came out of hiding and ran to the brink of the pit. They brandished triumphant fists, like hunters who have snared a bear. Then as he went on shouting – "Get me out! Pull me up! For pity's sake, help me!" – they began to throw things down on to him – the bedspread, the sheets, the pillows. They ripped apart the bed and threw it down, bit by bit, on to Ethelbert. Soon no more sound came from the well.

"Haul up the body, cut off his head, and bury him somewhere out of the way," said Queen Drida.

Offa no sooner learned what his wife had done, than the servants came running to him in terror, speaking of lights shining in the dark – lights which hovered over a piece of newly turned earth, lights marking a murdered man's grave. Offa went to see for himself, and sure enough, lights hung like altar candles over the place where the body and head of King Ethelbert had been hurriedly crammed underground. In a guilty panic, Offa told the servants to bury the remains somewhere else, before the lights attracted attention. But within hours the men were back, banging on his door, shouting in hoarse whispers that the lights were shining now over the new burial place.

That was when the real terror began – the guilt which troubled Offa's sleeping and waking hours. "Drida, you have made a murderer of me!" he said. "You and your scheming and ambition! How will we ever be clean of this good man's blood?"

The Queen gave a petulant shrug.

Offa covered his head with his hands. "But Drida! Alfleda loved him! She *wanted* to marry him. And now he is dead!"

Again that pettish shrug. "She's not my daughter, she's yours. I never liked her. Why should that simpering girl get what she wants? Do I? What has she ever done to deserve a beautiful young man like that? She's always been a thorn in my side, with her sheep's eyes and praying hands and hair like a yard of weak ale. I cannot abide her. Better she should be married to someone far away. On the other side of the . . ."

Offa did not stay to hear more. He ran from the room, sickened by the jealousy of his spoiled wife. He ran to his Bible, but found no comfort there. He ran to his confessor, but his confessor blanched white as a ghost. Offa's conscience was as bad as if he had done the deed himself. His dreams ran red with blood. The eerie, hovering lights beckoned him back time and time again to the place where Ethelbert lay; they even escorted the body as Offa removed it to a place of honour in Hereford Cathedral.

So ignoring his wife's shrill complaints, Offa set off on a journey far longer than Ethelbert's. He set off for Rome, to do penance for the death of an innocent man and to beg forgiveness from the Pope. And when he returned, he could be found, on many and many a day, crouched beside the dead King's tomb, recounting all that he had seen and done in the Eternal City.

The bronze likeness of the young dead King listened, holding his severed head in his lap, erect and serene, though with an expression of wistful sadness, perhaps at all pleasures of life which he had died too soon to enjoy.

In the course of his long reign (almost forty years), Offa expanded his kingdom from Mercia to encompass Kent, Sussex, Wessex and East Anglia, making him the most powerful monarch prior to AD 1000. He called himself *rex Anglorum*: the King of the English.

Versions of the story of Ethelbert and Alfleda (or Alfrida) vary so widely that there is probably little truth in the details. In another telling, a nobleman called Winebert beheads Ethelbert the moment he steps through Offa's door. But quite possibly Offa did assassinate this rival monarch for political reasons. The murdered King was certainly declared a saint.

The achievement for which Offa is best remembered is the building of a 100-kilometre-long earthwork – Offa's Dyke – as a defence against Welsh raiders with whom he spent his whole time at war. After his death, his kingdom fragmented again.

The Kingly Martyr
869

Instead of white gulls, black ravens were flying that summer over the eastern coast: the raven banners of Vikings. They swooped in across the ocean and gorged on Christian blood. Monasteries were sacked for the sake of their holy treasures, and villages burned for the sheer pleasure of destruction. Only King Edmund of East Anglia stood between his people and the Vikings. But Edmund's faith burned within him like the candle in the sanctuary which, by day or night, never goes out. He did not believe for a moment that God would suffer the true religion of Christ to be snuffed out by pagans.

So, as the Viking cleavers sliced through the November air, and the banner of the cross fell to an unkindness of ravens, what thoughts passed through the King's mind? He was defeated. His knights lay dead around him. His own life was at the mercy of a Viking warlord.

The Viking leader eyed his prisoner like a bird of prey. His eyes were paler than water. He had a certain respect for the King of this flat, damp, fertile kingdom. "You fought well. You are not dishonoured by defeat, King Edmund. I may yet spare your life."

No change of expression crossed Edmund's battle-weary face, but a flicker of hope must have kindled painfully in his heart.

"Yes, you shall go free – why not?" said his captor, spreading his hands in a gesture of generosity.

"Just forswear that milksop religion of yours and honour the Norse warrior gods who overthrew you today."

Edmund's head dropped forward. "I will never renounce my faith in Christ Jesus."

The pale yellow moustache rucked into a sneer, and the Viking slouched sideways in his chair. "Take him out and let the archers put him to some use."

Edmund was dragged roughly away, the guards snatching off his cuirass and shirt as they went. They tied him to a tree, and he saw the Viking archers restringing their longbows. It was late November: his bare limbs jumped with cold.

"There is still time to change banners!" called the man with pale blue eyes. "What has he ever done for you, this Christ? This Jesus Christ?"

"He has blessed my soul with bliss, as I pray He will one day bless yours," said Edmund. "I forgive you this spilling of my blood."

The Viking leader turned away with disgust and vexation. As he went, he could hear the whisk of arrows through the leaves, the thud of arrowheads sinking into the tree's trunk. Then the archers found their distance, and began to hit their mark. It gave him no satisfaction.

When the arrows had finally killed Edmund, his head was cut off, and the Vikings moved on to lay waste to more kingdoms. The King's followers, reeling with horror, despair and fatigue, emerged from hiding. But though they were able to cut down the body bristling with arrows, they could not find his head. For days they searched, but without success.

As they combed Eglesdane Wood one last time, a voice called out: "*Over here!*" Everyone asked everyone else. "Was that you?"

Then the voice came again. "*I am here! This way! Over here!*" Their hair stood on end.

Following the voice, they came to a clearing. Then a dozen men gasped and froze, their hands on their sword hilts. There stood a huge wolf, grey as winter, its front paws straddling the bloody head, its lower jaw resting on the pale forehead of the martyr-King. They waited for it to spring, but the wolf backed grudgingly away from its prize, as though it had merely been waiting for them to come. A page darted forward and grabbed up the head, but the wolf did not move to recapture it, nor to run away. Hastily the King's party beat back through the woods. Walking, they broke into a run as they realized the wolf was dogging their footsteps, keeping the scent of them in its nostrils, watching them with its yellow eyes. But they got back safely to the body of the dead King. Now he could be laid to rest.

They took him to Hoxne. And every time they looked back, the wolf was still following, loping along after the horses, melting into the trees if they reined in.

Word of Edmund's death was spreading – not of his defeat, but of his marvellous courage, his saintly faith. Edmund their king had gone to join the saints. Now there was one more saint in heaven to watch over the people of Anglia.

As the sorry remains, body and head, were lowered into the grave, an uninvited guest stood watching from the church lych-gate. With watchful eyes, the wolf observed the laying to rest of the dead King. Only then did it turn and lope back into the forest whose trees, in the rising wind, whispered a thousand prayers for the soul of St Edmund.

The name of Bury St Edmunds bears witness to the final place of the martyred king. His bones were moved there after a miracle cult grew up around his memory. He was probably about twenty-nine years old when he died.

Tradition has it that King Offa, who had no son of his own, adopted Edmund, the son of a Frankish king, to be his heir. Little else is known about him.

Alfred and the Cakes

878

Alfred the Great of Wessex had for his ancestors three of the ancient Saxon gods: Woden, Sceaf and Geat. So when Saxon Britain began to fall, field by town, to the invading Danes, Alfred and his brother Aethelred went out to fight them. In 871, at the battle of Ashdown, the marauders were routed for the first time.

It was a hard won victory. Though their muscles should have ached with exhaustion, success lent the Saxon troops new energy. They set about hewing and gouging the hillside nearby as they had hewn and gouged the Danes, carving out the shape of a gigantic white horse in the chalkstone, for future generations to see and remember.

But the Danes came back again and again. They killed Aethelred and cowed the Saxons to such an extent that they abandoned their king. Along with a few loyal men, Alfred alone held out against them, a mysterious figure living a shifting, ghostly life, haunting the countryside, emerging from hiding to attack the Danes.

By 878, things were going so badly that Alfred's pocket army was confined to the Isle of Athelney in the middle of the Summer Land. Their shelter was in turf cottages and their food was bread made from acorns grubbed from under the spreading oak trees.

Alfred sought shelter from a local man – a cowherd – and asked whether he might sleep a night or two at his house.

"By all that's holy, my little place ain no fit shelter for a king, sire! But you'z honour me and the wife past all speaking, if you'z see fit to sleep under our roof!"

Denewulf was not exaggerating: his little turf-roofed house was mean and small and bare. But Alfred was simply glad to be out of the rain. He had no fear for his safety among these good people: they were all ready to lay down their lives for the Saxon cause. This cowherd, for instance. He would return the man's loyalty if ever it were within his power to do so.

With much bowing and blushing – "My wife – where is the silly woman? – she'll make you some food – prepare you up a bed" – Denewulf seated Alfred on a rush stool in front of the fire and dashed away again to try to find his wife and tell her the wonderful honour which had befallen them. Alfred spread out his great swordsman's hands to warm them at the grate.

"What you'm doing in here soaking up th'heat?" asked an imperious voice behind him.

Alfred turned round and caught his first sight of the cowherd's wife. "Your husband said I might stay here for a while."

"Oh yes, that be typical of 'im, the lummock." The woman had never seen a king before. She did not see a king now – only some mud-stained, unkempt ragamuffin with leaves in his hair, sitting on her best rush stool. "Well, you'm best make yourself useful. Can you do that?" she snapped. "Shake the blankets? Sweep out the straw?"

The King had never been asked such a thing before.

"I expect so."

Alfred was dog-tired, but he was also a gentleman. So he did as he was told, and thanked the lady when she brought him a bite of food. Her manners were not quite those of a royal valet, nor was bread and cheese exactly a banquet, but Alfred was used to less. He realized that the woman had no idea who he was.

He marvelled at the bareness of her existence – the few sticks of furniture, the empty store cupboard, the single cooking pot. But he marvelled, too, at the way she could whip up an egg, a spoon of flour and honey into a cake-mix, and set the little scones to bake on a griddle over a twig fire.

"Now you'm watch them cakes and don't you'm take youz eyes off 'em, or I'll have words to say!" barked the woman. "I have to milk the cows. Someone has to . . . And *no nibbling*, you hear?" were her parting words.

Alfred smiled to himself, then settled down in front of the hearth, legs stretched out, and watched the cakes. Little bubbles rose up to the surface of each scone and popped with a sigh. They swelled, as if with Saxon pride . . .

As he sat, Alfred sank into thinking, remembering the bad times, remembering the good.

One day, in the forests, he had come across a lady in blue standing very still in a downshaft of sunlight. "Are you lost, lady?" he had asked. But when she turned towards him, he had known in an instant, with absolute certainty, that he was looking at Mary, mother of Jesus, at the Holy Madonna herself. Speechless with awe, Alfred had done the only thing his wits would allow, and cast at her feet the most precious object he

was carrying – his jewelled cloak pin. Before
disappearing like a summer mirage, the lady had
opened her lips and said . . .

"You goon! You great lazy, idle, good-for-nothing
lummock! You let my cakes burn!" Alfred slipped off
his stool in waking and peered around him: the hut was
oddly dark. It seemed to be full of smoke. "You great
hulking fool of a wet Wednesday! What you got for
brains, frogspawn or mud?" Six smouldering little
cakes reproached him from the griddle, as black and
brittle as charcoal.

"I'm –"

"I know what *you* be," the woman went on. "Anyone can see what *you* be! You be your mother's greatest shame and your father's worst mistake! You be a wet cloud looking for someone like me to rain on! What *you* be is –"

"The King of Wessex," said a voice behind her. Her husband, the cowherd, stood in the doorway, paler than the pail of milk he was carrying. But it was not he who had spoken. It was one of the officers behind him, cloaks thrown back off their mail shirts, swords drawn.

The woman's mouth froze in mid-word. "Son of Aethelwulf," the officer went on. "Kin to the gods Woden, Sceaf and Geat; Lord of Wessex. What shall I do with her, sire?"

The woman's mouth still spoke its small, silent "O". Her eyes filled with tears. Now she would be hanged, and her hut burned down, and her husband's cattle forfeit to the army. Now she would be cursed by her neighbours, remembered as the shrew who had bad-mouthed the greatest man in England. She fell to her knees and curled her body into a crouching bow. She could find no words to excuse her offence.

Alfred picked up a cake and burnt his fingers doing it. He smiled to himself and then at the others. "Why, help her to her feet, man! She's perfectly right! This good woman left me to mind her cakes, and I let them burn. She's quite right – I am a fool! Shall I hang her for telling me the simple truth? Here, madam." He pulled out his purse. "Here's recompense for the cakes, and a little something for your . . . honest and fearless nature. Now gentlemen! Let's sit and discuss what can be done to pull England from the fire before she burns, shall we?"

It is unlikely that the White Horse at Uffington was carved in celebration of the victory at Ashdown. It probably represents a Celtic god. The Alfred Jewel, on the other hand, found near Athelney in 1693 and bearing the words (in Latin) "Alfred had me made", could well be the cloak pin referred to in the legend of the Virgin Mary.

Alfred's greatest success came at Ethandune, when he defeated Guthrum the Dane. At the Peace of Wedmore which followed, the Danes agreed to withdraw to the other side of a line formed by the River Thames and the old Roman road Watling Street. All the land to the north of this line would be theirs (the Danelaw), while Alfred could keep Wessex and London. So England was now shared between Saxon and Dane.

Dunstan and the Devil

about 980

There was a man who lived through the reigns of eight kings, and lent his advice to six of them. Small wonder that kings and nobles held no dread for him. St Dunstan was of the opinion that God was on his side, and that made him a dangerous man to cross. His enemies said he dabbled in the black arts – and that made him more dangerous still.

As a young man, he was by trade a blacksmith – or perhaps it was merely a hobby of his, for later, when King Edmund made him Abbot of Glastonbury, he set up a forge in a little stone cell projecting from the outer wall of the abbey and would go there, by way of relaxation, to forge horseshoes and pokers and scythes. Local people would call on him and ask him, "Make me this, Father Abbot," or "Make me that."

One day an uncommonly pretty woman came and fluttered her lashes at Dunstan, asking if he would make her a toasting fork. While he worked, she moved about the room – a flick of the hips, a flash of the eyes, a smile. But Dunstan kept his eyes firmly on his work. The hammer clanged down. Sparks exploded: there was a smell of sulphur. The woman became still more daring, brushing up against him, fingering his tonsure. It was only as she stepped over a hammer on the floor that her skirts lifted, and Dunstan glimpsed her feet.

Lifting his blacksmith's tongs red-hot from the furnace, he reached out with them – and seized the woman by the nose!

How she shrieked and screamed. But Dunstan did not let go. How she altered into a mottled, bent old crone gripped in the lips of the red-hot pincers. But still Dunstan did not let go. Now she was not even female, but a sooty writhing fellow roaring and trumpeting in the grip of the tongs. But Dunstan still did not let go – no, not even when the Devil himself was dancing in front of Dunstan on his two cloven hooves.

"You should not have let me see your feet," said Dunstan smiling grimly. Then he threw the Devil out of the window, just as the bells rang for vespers.

The Devil was a fool, really, to approach Dunstan in the shape of a woman. For women were not a breed St Dunstan much cared for. In those days, it was the custom for certain orders of priests to marry and have families. But Dunstan thought the whole priesthood should stay unmarried. The arguments had been dragging on, bitter and unresolved, for many years when, one day, a meeting took place in an upstairs room at Calne in Wiltshire.

Opinions were equally split. It was hard to see how a final decision could be reached. Dunstan closed the proceedings. "We shall never agree, so I say, let the decision rest with Christ Jesus Himself!"

There was an ominous groaning of timbers. Then a large portion of the floor suddenly fell away, and the long central table listed and slid through the hole like a

sinking ship, carrying with it everyone on one side of the room.

It was a long drop. In the room below, some lay trapped under the table or under fallen roofbeams. Some staggered ghostly white from the ruins, showered with plaster. Dunstan and his followers, however, were left in the upper room, like angels looking down on the chaos below.

Dunstan's enemies said he had sabotaged the floor. Dunstan said that God had taken a hand. And even if dry rot were really to blame, still Dunstan carried the day. Marriage was forbidden to the clergy.

Not that some monks cared what Dunstan said. Some monks did not give a fig for the holy life or their vows of poverty and virtue. The monks of Middle Fen,

for instance. Their lives were as easy and pleasant as they could make them, and they never gave God or religion a thought from one day's end to the next. Their wives and children, sweethearts and friends all lived together in the abbey which stood on an island in the midst of Middle Fen – a rowdy, lawless rabble with wine-stains on their habits and money on their minds.

But Dunstan came down on them like the wrath of God. No sermons or penances. No fines or trials. He simply turned them into eels, every one, and emptied them into the rivers and dikes and ponds and marshes of the fenland. That's why the place is called Ely – the place of eels – and why Dunstan is better remembered than any of the kings he served.

Dunstan was, in his time, Abbot of Glastonbury, Bishop of Worcester, Bishop of London and Archbishop of Canterbury. His career rick-racked between high power and obscurity as a succession of rival kings either relied on his advice or chased him out of the country. As a young man he was banished for practising unlawful arts - which probably means he was an experimental scientist.

When King Edward was murdered in 978 and Aethelred was crowned in his place, Dunstan's political career was over: Aethelred hated him. Dunstan died in isolation ten years later but obtained the ultimate honour of being made a saint.

London Bridge is Falling Down

1013 and 1016

"The Vikings are coming! the Vikings are coming!" The cry had echoed so often up the river reaches, and yet it never failed to terrify. London was the great prize in the game, and London was being captured and recaptured now like a carcass of meat wrangled over by lions.

In 1013, King Swayne the Dane had taken the city from King Ethelred, but Ethelred was determined to take it back. He enlisted the help of King Olaf of Norway, and sailed up the Thames estuary – more dragon-headed ships lunging upstream, more cries of "The Vikings are coming!"

Swayne was ready for them. His men were massed on London Bridge, at their feet lay huge cairns of rock for pelting the attacking ships. There were archers, too, and spear-wielders.

But Ethelred knew the river: it was *his* river. He had foreseen the blockade, and equipped Olaf's ships accordingly, each with a high platform rising from the foredeck.

"He thinks to shield his rowers from the rocks," thought Swayne, peering against the brightness of the river. "It is protection for the rowers."

But as the dragon-prows nosed closer, Ethelred's and

Olaf's men swarmed up on to the platforms so as to stand almost on a level with their opponents on the bridge. They stood in pairs, one holding a coil of rope tipped with a grappling hook, the other holding a shield with which to fend off the arrows, the stones, the spears.

Insanely, it seemed as if they would really moor up to the bridge, for they pitched their grappling irons at the bridge's wooden pilings.

Their faces were on a level with the bridge parapet: like sailors in two closing warships, both sides looked each other in the eye. There was a moment's silence, like a pause to draw breath. Then the men on the bridge were hurling, shouting, bloodying their hands on the large rocks in their haste to heave them over on to the ships beneath.

Six, a dozen, twenty of the men on the platforms were dislodged by stones and plunged into the river. Some fell stunned to the decking. But then the rowers swung their legs over the benches and faced the other way. The dragon-headed ships dropped back downstream, but between them and the bridge now ran a dozen stout ropes.

"Heave!" cried Ethelred.

"Heave!" cried Olaf. And the rowers heaved till the muscles stood proud of their shoulders. The ropes twanged taut, spraying silver droplets into the air.

The grappling irons chewed on the wood of the bridge; two broke free and splashed into the river, but the rest held. The strain stirred the wooden pilings of the bridge in their muddy sockets in the river bed.

What with the great weight of stones amassed on the wooden planking and the great press of defenders, the bridge was already overladen. Now, as its pilings were dragged out from under it, London Bridge broke its wooden back.

For a moment it staggered drunkenly on its unsteady legs. Then down into the Thames fell stones and shields, timber and helmets and men. The dragon-headed longships rolled on the huge wave which washed downstream from the splash, and the rowers rested on their oars as silence fell over the wide, grey river.

Within three years another king held London – Edmund Ironside – and London Bridge had been built up again, too strongly for whole galleys of rowers to pull it down. But King Canute was a man who did not pit brawn against brawn. He brought the power of cunning to the problem of capturing London.

Arming his men with picks and shovels in place of swords, he had them dig. He had them dig a channel just a hand-span wider than the beam of his ships. It ran south from the Thames. Then west. It bypassed London, looping to the south, and, when flooded with Thames water from either end, it filled to a depth just a hand-span deeper than the draw of Canute's ships. Long chains of men, heaving like barge horses on cables of rope, hauled the entire navy of Canute round Edmund Ironside's London, and attacked from the west – from inland! – unexpected, unresisted, irresistible.

When King Swayne attacked England in 1013 he was accompanied by his son. A few years later, that son had become king of Denmark, and as Canute the Great came back to finish the job. He was England's first Viking king, capturing the country from Ethelred (or Aethelred) "the Unready" in 1015 – all except for London, which was held by Ethelred's son and heir, Edmund Ironside. Hence this masterly stroke of engineering and military tactics.

Ultimately, Knut reached an agreement with Edmund Ironside to share the kingdom, but Edmund died a month later and everything fell to Knut. To strengthen his claim to the throne, he set aside his so-called "northern wife", Aelgifu, and married King Ethelred's widow, Emma.

Also by Geraldine McCaughrean
Illustrated by Richard Brassey

◆━━━━━━━━━━━━━◆

Britannia

◆━━━━━━━━━━━━━◆

100 Great Stories from
British History

In one volume illustrated in full colour on every
page, this unique book comprises a hundred
stories from the very beginnings of British
history right up to the end of the twentieth
century. Many are more legendary than
historically accurate, and Geraldine
McCaughrean has chosen them simply because
they are wonderful stories that have been
known and loved for generations and give us a
sense of our past.

A panel giving the facts behind the stories
accompanies each one, and there is an
introduction, an index, and a list of
recommended reading.

Britannia on Stage

Geraldine McCaughrean has turned twenty-five of the stories from *Britannia* into short plays that are easy and fun for children at top primary and secondary level to perform. They are short enough to be read or performed in class, but she has also provided a framework so several plays can be acted together to make a whole performance. There are simple stage directions and suggestions for a few basic props and costumes, and a programme note on each play gives the background to the story.

Very lively, with lots of action and a chance for as many or as few children to perform as necessary, the plays are also a great read, and the line drawings by Richard Brassey are as entertaining as his pictures for the original *Britannia*.